Portraits

of

the

Great

and

Famous

THOMAS CRAWFORD

WORKBOOK PRESS LLC
187 E Warm Springs Rd,
Suite B285, Las Vegas, NV 89119, USA

Website: https://workbookpress.com/
Hotline: 1-888-818-4856
Email: admin@workbookpress.com

Ordering Information:
Quantity sales. Special discounts are available on quantity purchases by corporations, associations, and others.
For details, contact the publisher at the address above.

ISBN-13:   000-0-000000-00-0 (Paperback Version)
                    000-0-000000-00-0 (Digital Version)

REV. DATE: 03/31/2022

PORTRAITS

By Thomas Crawford

Dedicated to Caroline
and to Hardy, Martha and Caitlin

INTRODUCTION

The twenty-one people here portrayed represent the highest qualities of character and achievement. The group is not "the ideal," except to the extent that it is worthy of that tribute by my personal standards. You might select a different group of people to honor. I chose this group in part because of the great pleasure I took in painting their portraits.

Abraham Lincoln, Ida Wells , Frederick Douglass, Thurgood Marshall and Martin Luther King, Jr. are easily linked by their impassioned crusades for racial justice and equality. Ruth Bader Ginsburg is included for her tireless advocacy for women's rights and for social justice for all.

Herman Melville, Mark Twain and Albert Camus are pre-eminent writers and seekers of truth. Journalists Jessica Mitford and I.F. Stone influenced public action and social reform for the public good. Vincent Van Gogh, the incomparable modern painter, and the musicians, Enrico Caruso, Renata Tebaldi, Billie Holiday and Giuseppe Verdi arouse our deepest feelings and aspirations with the beauty of their art.

Fidel Castro has done more than anyone to foil U.S. Imperialism in Latin America. And, four great athletes Satchel Paige, Jackie Robinson, Muhammad Ali and Roger Federer deserve our respect for their unmatched grace and prowess.

–Thomas Crawford

ABRAHAM LINCOLN

b. February 12, 1809, Hodgenville, KY; d. April 15, 1865, Washington, D.C.

Born in a one-room log cabin, Lincoln was a self-educated lawyer who reportedly said, "I studied with nobody." He was elected 16th President of the United States in 1860 precipitating the secession of seven southern slave states and the formation of the Confederacy, even before Lincoln moved into the White House. He guided the North to victory in the Civil War while his efforts to end slavery included the Emancipation Proclamation of 1863 and the passage of the Thirteenth Amendment to the Constitution outlawing slavery. Lincoln was assassinated by John Wilkes Booth five days after Confederate General Robert E. Lee surrendered to Union General Ulysses S. Grant. Any attempted tribute to the greatest American must fail as puny and inadequate in comparison to Lincoln's own words in the Gettysburg Address:

"Fourscore and seven years ago our fathers brought forth, on this continent, a new nation, conceived in liberty, and dedicated to the proposition that all men are created equal. Now we are engaged in a great civil war, testing whether that nation, or any nation so conceived, and so dedicated, can long endure. We are met on a great battlefield of that war. We have come to dedicate a portion of that field, as a final resting-place for those who here gave their lives, that that nation might live. It is altogether fitting and proper that we should do this. But, in a larger sense, we cannot dedicate, we cannot consecrate – we cannot hallow – this ground. The brave men, living and dead, who struggled here, have consecrated it far above our poor power to add or detract. The world will little note, nor long remember, what we say here, but it can never forget what they did here. It is for us the living, rather, to be dedicated here to the unfinished work which they who fought here have thus far so nobly advanced. It is rather for us to be here dedicated to the great task remaining before us – that from these honored dead we take increased devotion to that cause for which they here gave the last full measure of devotion – that we here highly resolve that these dead shall not have died in vain – that this nation, under God, shall have a new birth of freedom, and that government of the people, by the people, for the people, shall not perish from the earth."

IDA B. WELLS
b. July 16, 1809, Holly Springs, MI; d. March 25, 1931, Chicago, IL

Born into slavery and freed by the Civil War, Ida Wells was probably the most famous black American woman during her lifetime. Her parents and an infant sibling died in a yellow fever epidemic that ravaged her hometown while Ida and five younger siblings were visiting their grandmother elsewhere in Mississippi. Thereafter, Ida kept and cared for her siblings as she taught school and attended college. While teaching she also wrote editorials about race issues for a Washington, D.C., newspaper.

In 1889 she became co-owner and editor of an anti-segregation newspaper in Memphis. That same year a friend and two companions were lynched in Memphis by a white mob. Ida Wells urged black people to leave Memphis and in response more than 6,000 black residents left the city in protest. In 1892 a white mob destroyed her newspaper office. Wells left Memphis and moved to Chicago, where she continued her campaigns against racial injustice. That same year, she published what is probably her single most significant writing, "Southern Horrors: Lynch Law in all Its Phases." She introduced the study saying: "It is with no pleasure that I have dipped my hands in the corruption here exposed...Somebody must show that the African-American race is more sinned against than sinning, and it seems to have fallen upon me to do so."

In 1895 she published *The Red Record*, a 100-page pamphlet documenting lynching in the U.S.A. since the Emancipation Proclamation of 1863. She estimated that from 1863 to 1895 "ten thousand Negroes have been killed in cold blood [through lynching] without the formality of a judicial trial and legal execution."

GIUSEPPE VERDI
b. October 10,1813, La Roncole, Italy; d. 1901, Milano, Italy.

Generally considered the greatest Italian opera composer, Verdi came after Bellini, Donizetti and Rossini and preceded Puccini. His early work, notably *Nabucco* (1847), reflected his sympathy with the Risorgimento movement seeking the reunification of Italy. In that early period he also composed *Macbeth* (1847) and *Luisa Miller* (1849). In a remarkable six year period of creativity Verdi composed *Rigoletto* (1851), *Il trovatore* (1853), *La traviata* (1853), and *Simon Boccanegra* (1857). That was followed by *Un ballo in maschera* (1859), *La forza del destino* (1862), *Don Carlos* (1867) and *Aida* (1871). In the late period of his work Verdi composed his Requiem mass (1874), and the operas *Otello* (1887) and *Falstaff* (1893). His brilliant librettists were Maria Piave for *Rigoletto* and *La traviata*, and Arrigo Boito for *Otello* and *Falstaff.*

FREDERICK DOUGLASS
b.1818, Talbot County, Maryland; d.1895, Washington, D.C.

Born into slavery, Douglass was of mixed race (Native American, African and European). He did not know his father but assumed that he was his master. He was separated from his mother as an infant and wrote in his biography, "I do not recollect ever seeing my mother by the light of day...She would lie down with me, and get me to sleep, but before I waked she was gone." Douglass was twenty when he escaped from slavery in Maryland to freedom in New York.

Frederick Douglass was arguably the most influential African-American of the nineteenth century because of his brilliant oratory and incisive antislavery writings. He was the leading abolitionist of his time and a national leader of various reform causes including women's rights, temperance, peace, land reform, free public education and the abolition of capital punishment. His greatness can be best appreciated today by a reading of his three biographies: *Narrative of the Life of Frederick Douglass* (1845), *My Bondage and My Freedom* (1855), and *Life and Times of Frederick Douglass* (1881, and 1892 revision).

He said or wrote:

"It is easier to build strong children than to repair broken men."
"What, to the American slave, is your Fourth of July? I answer: A day that reveals to him, more than all other days in the year, the gross injustice and cruelty to which he is the constant victim. To him your celebration is a sham."
"In all the relations of life and death, we are met by the color line."

HERMAN MELVILLE
b. August 1, 1819, NY; d. 1891, NY.

Melville's first book, *Typee*, an account of his experiences in Polynesia published in 1846, was an international best seller, but his masterpiece, *Moby Dick*, an epic story of a whaling voyage, (published in 1851), was not an immediate success. The author and his writings were largely forgotten for thirty years after his death until critical attention and popular interest in his art were revived. Today few critics fail to include Herman Melville among the pre-eminent novelists of the world or recognize *Moby Dick* as one of the greatest prose works in all of English literature. In addition to *Redburn* (1849), about life on a merchant ship and *White Jacket,* (1850) about life aboard a man-of-war, Melville is justly celebrated for other distinguished works of fiction, including: *Bartleby the Scrivner* (1853), *The Encantadas* (1854) and *Benito Cereno* (1855), all collected in 1856 in *The Piazza Tales*; and *The Confidence Man* (1857). The much adapted novella, *Billy Budd*, was posthumously published in 1857.

He wrote:
In *Moby Dick*: "I love to sail forbidden seas, and land on barbarous coasts."
""Better sleep with a cannibal than a drunken Christian."
"A whale-ship was my Yale College and my Harvard."
"For as this appalling ocean surrounds the verdant land, so in the soul of man there lies one insular Tahiti, full of peace and joy, but encompassed by all the horrors of the half-known life."
In *The Confidence Man*: "What is an atheist but one who does not, or will not, see in the universe a ruling principle of love; and what is a misanthrope, but one who does not or will not see in man a ruling principle of kindness?"

MARK TWAIN
b. November 30, 1835, Florida, MO; d. 1910, Redding, CT

Samuel Langhorne Clemens, known by his pen name, Mark Twain, wrote *The Adventures of Huckleberry Finn, The Adventures of Tom Sawyer, Life on the Mississippi, Roughing It, The Innocents Abroad*, and the short story, "The Jumping Frog of Calaveras County." Twain grew up in Hannibal, Missouri, a port town on the Mississippi River. He left school after the fifth grade and educated himself in public libraries while working as a typesetter and printer. He became a river boat pilot and worked at that highly specialized and well-paid vocation until 1861 when the Civil War broke out. He moved West, joining his brother who was secretary to the governor of the Nevada Territory. He roughed it for several years and ended up in San Francisco in 1864.

Twain's remarkable success as writer, humorist, lecturer and inventor resulted in lasting international fame and admiration. In 1965 the deposed president of the Dominican Republic, Juan Bosch, was prevented by the U.S. government from returning to his own country to join the revolution being fought in his name. A journalist asked if he was an enemy of the United States. Bosch replied, "No. Only an enemy of U.S. imperialism. No one who has read Mark Twain can be an enemy of the United States."

VINCENT VAN GOGH
b.1853, Groot Zundert, Holland; d.1890, Auvers-sur-Oise, France

Van Gogh was twenty-seven when he decided to be a painter. He took his own life 10 years later. During that brief period he developed from a draftsman of grim scenes of the poor and oppressed to become the father of modern Expressionism and a painter of extreme originality whose distinctive brush strokes and vibrant palette seemed to be influenced by no one or nothing but Van Gogh himself. Among his masterpieces are Pere Tanguy (Collection Stavros Niarchos, Athens); L'Arlesienne (Metropolitan Museum of Art, New York); The Starry Night (Museum of Modern Art, New York); The Road Menders (Cleveland Museum of Art).

ENRICO CARUSO
b. 1873, Naples, Italy; d. 1921, Naples, Italy

His debut in Naples, 1894, in Morelli's *L'amico Francesco*, led to engagements all over Italy, including La Scala, 1900, when he first appeared as Nemorino (*L'Elisir d' Amore*). He made his debut at Covent Garden in 1902; and as the Duke (*Rigoletto*) in 1903 at the Met, where he sang for 18 seasons. He created the tenor roles in *Fedora*, *Adriana Lecouvreur*, *Germania*, and *La Fanciulla del West*. He built a repertory of approximately 50 roles, both lyric and dramatic. A great recording artist, he was the archtypal tenor of the 20th century and probably the most famous singer of all time.

LEROY "SATCHEL" PAIGE
b. 1906, Mobile, AL; d. 1982, Kansas City, MO.

Satchel Paige became a forty-two-year-old Major Leaguer in 1948. He and his white counterpart, Babe Ruth, were undisputedly baseball's greatest gate attractions, Paige as pitcher and Ruth as slugger. When I was eleven in 1949 and a batboy for the World Champion Cleveland Indians, I met Paige at a spring training game played against the St. Louis Browns in Burbank, California. At the time I was more interested in Boudreau, Doby and Feller but even then I saw that his own teammates seemed to be in awe of the "old" pitcher.

Because Paige played most of his career in the Negro Leagues and barnstorming in the U.S., Puerto Rico, Cuba, the Dominican Republic and Mexico, accurate statistics are not available. Nonetheless, creditable estimates place his winning games at more than 2,000. His fastball, hesitation pitch and an array of other pitches are legendary.

He is fondly remembered for his advice on how to stay young:

1) Avoid fried meats, which angry up the blood.
2) If your stomach disputes you, lie down and pacify it with cool thoughts.
3) Keep the juices flowing by jangling around gently as you move.
4) Go very light on the vices, such as carrying on in society.
   The social ramble ain't restful.
5) Avoid running at all times.
6) Don't look back. Something might be gaining on you.

ISADORE FEINSTEIN STONE
b. December 24, 1907, Philadelphia, PA; d. 1989, Boston, MA

I. F. Stone, a radical investigative journalist who liked to be called Izzy, is best remembered for his self-published newsletter, the I.F. Stone Weekly. NYU's journalism department ranked the newsletter in sixteenth place among "The Top 100 Works of Journalism in the U.S. in the 20th Century," and second among print journalism publications.

Stone dropped out of the University of Pennsylvania to work for *The Philadelphia Inquirer*, then quit to join the *Inquirer*'s rival, *The Philadelphia Record*, then moved to the *New York Post*, the *The Nation magazine*, and others. In 1950 Stone found himself blacklisted and unable to get work because of McCarthyism. At that point he established *The I. F. Stone Weekly*. The best way to savor Stone's reportage today is through his books, including *The I.F. Stone's Weekly Reader*; *The War Years 1939-1945*; *The Hidden History of the Korean War*; *The Truman Era 1945-1952*; *The Haunted Fifties*; *In A Time of Torment*; *Polemics and Prophecies 1967-1970*; and *The Best of I.F. Stone.*

Over the years, Stone was ahead of most prominent journalists in seeing the virtues of the most "progressive" solutions to global problems. As a Jew he was a moderate Zionist supporting the state of Israel, but sympathetic to Arab resistance to their physical dispossession and favored a one-state solution. In the 1950s he was probably the most persistent critic of McCarthy. He exposed the U.S. Government's propaganda campaign depicting the Korean conflict as an international communist conspiracy, and he was one of the earliest and most effective critics of the U.S. misadventure in Vietnam.

THURGOOD MARSHALL
b.July 2, 1908, Baltimore, MD; d. 1993, Bethesda, MD

Thurgood Marshall was the first African-American appointed to the U.S. Supreme Court. He graduated first in his class at Howard University School of Law in 1933. After graduation he began a twenty-fifth-year affiliation with the NAACP and in 1940 founded and became the executive director of the NAACP Legal Defense and Education Fund. In that position he argued and won twenty-nine of thirty two cases before the U.S. Supreme Court, including *Shelley v. Kramer 334 U.S. 1* (1948); *Sweatt v. Painter 339 U.S. 629* (1950); *McLaurin v. Oklahoma State Regents 339 U.S. 637* (1950); and *Brown v. Board of Education of Topeka 347 U.S. 483* (1954), in which the Court held that racially separate education facilities are inherently not equal.

President John F. Kennedy appointed Marshall to the U.S. Court of Appeals for the Second Circuit in 1961. In 1965 President Lyndon B. Johnson appointed him to be the U.S. Solicitor General and then in 1967 elevated him to the U.S. Supreme Court, where he served for twenty-four years.

Justice Marshall and his principal ally on the U.S. Supreme Court, Justice William Brennan, consistently voted together to protect the rights of criminal suspects, to support abortion rights, and to oppose the death penalty.

ALBERT CAMUS
b. November 7, 1913, Algeria; d. 1960, VIlleblevin, France

Albert Camus was a novelist, playwright, essayist and philosopher whose ideas perhaps best addressed mankind's alienation and disillusionment in the post-World War II age. His novels, *L'etranger* (The Stranger), *La Peste* (The Plague), *La Chute* (The Fall) and his non-fiction works, *Le Mythe de Sisyphe,* (The Myth of Sisyphus) and *L'homme revolte* (The Rebel) earned him a Nobel Prize for Literature and a vast international readership.

Camus' s father was killed in World War I less than a year after his son was born. His mother, an illiterate house-cleaner, moved with her infant son to an impoverished working-class area of Algiers. Albert was a keen student and won a scholarship to the local lycee and then won admittance to the University of Algiers. After university, he worked as a journalist for a socialist paper and after WW II broke out Camus moved to France and joined the resistance movement, and during the German occupation worked as an editor for the underground Parisian daily, *Combat.*

When the Algerian War began in 1954, Camus was torn between the Algerian cause for autonomy, on one hand, and the French government's efforts to protect French citizens, like his mother living in Algeria, on the other hand. Behind the scenes, he worked for imprisoned Algerians facing the death penalty. In "Reflections on the Guillotine", Camus had this to say: "Capital punishment is the most premeditated of murders, to which no criminal's deed, however calculated, can be compared. For there to be an equivalency, the death penalty would have to punish a criminal who had warned his victim of the date on which he would inflict a horrible death on him and who, from that moment onward, had confined him at his mercy for months."

BILLIE HOLIDAY
b. April 7, 1915, Philadelphia, PA; d. 1959, New York, NY

Elenora Fagan, known as Billie Holiday, was born to her thirteen year-old mother and teenaged father, raised by a single parent and often left in the care of others, and dropped out of school at age eleven. She worked with her mother, first in Baltimore doing menial jobs and then in Harlem, New York, at age fourteen at a brothel. The brothel was raided and mother and daughter were both sent to prison. After release from prison, as a young teenager without formal music training, Billie began singing in Harlem night clubs. Her reputation gradually grew and in the years from 1931-35 her talent was recognized by prominent musicians, including Benny Goodman, Chick Webb and Fletcher Henderson. Her father, a musician, was performing with the Henderson band and Billie established a close and lasting relationship with him.

From 1935-38 Billie worked closely with four of the greatest jazz musicians, Teddy Wilson, Lester Young, Count Basie and Artie Shaw, and began her rise as a pre-eminent jazz vocalist. In 1939 she recorded and performed "Strange Fruit" in inimitable fashion that will forever be the acme of anti-racist jazz. During the war years she performed and recorded incomparable versions of "I Cover the Waterfront," "I'll Get By," "He's Funny That Way," "I'll Be Seeing You," "Embraceable You," "God Bless the Child" (she co-wrote the song), "Lover Man," "That Ole Devil Called Love," and "Good Morning Heartache."

Billie takes her place beside Ella Fitzgerald as perhaps the best jazz singer ever. Listeners slightly partial to Billie's contralto voice can be understood for judging her singing to be peerless for phrasing, feeling and improvisation. Frank Sinatra said in a 1958 *Ebony* magazine interview: "Billie Holiday...was, and still remains, the greatest single musical influence on me."

JESSICA MITFORD

b. September 11, 1917, Glouchestershire, England; d. 1996, Oakland, CA

Jessica Mitford, called "Decca," was the youngest of six daughters born to an aristocratic British family. She grew up in a series of her father's houses and had little formal education but was widely read. Two of her sisters were supporters of Hitler, and a third, Nancy Mitford, was a writer and author of the novel *Love in a Cold Climate*. Decca was first a communist and then a socialist. Her first husband, Edmond Romilly, a nephew of Winston Churchill, was killed in 1941 when the Royal Canadian Air Force plane he was piloting was shot down.

Mitford migrated to the U.S. and in 1945 married Robert Treuhaft, who became a criminal defense and civil rights lawyer in Oakland, California. For years, often while working with her husband, she was a civil rights advocate and investigative journalist while also writing several acclaimed books, including: *Hons and Rebels* (U.S. title, *Daughters and Rebels*, a memoir of growing up in an aristocratic household); *The American Way of Death*, about the funeral industry and unscrupulous practices against grieving families; *A Fine Old Conflict*, a comic memoir about joining then leaving the communist party.

J.K. Rowling, author of the Harry Potter series said, "My most influential writer, without doubt, is Jessica Mitford."

JACKIE ROBINSON
b. January 31, 1919, Cairo, GA; d. 1972, Stamford, CT

One can make the case that Jackie Robinson, the first African-American to play major league baseball, was the greatest American of the 20th century. In terms of civil rights and racial justice, he did more than anyone by his own actions and as an influence on the actions of others. His pride, courage and personal morality were at the highest level of humanity. He was probably the best all around athlete of our time – better than Jim Thorpe, Jim Brown or specialists like Michael Jordan, Pele and Babe Ruth.

Born in Georgia into a family of sharecroppers, Jackie, at age one, and four siblings moved with their mother to Pasadena, California. At John Muir High School he played five varsity sports and broke his older brother Mack's record in the long jump. (Mack was a silver medalist in the 200 meter race behind Jesse Owens in the 1936 Olympics in Berlin.) Jackie continued to compete in several sports at both Pasadena Junior College and UCLA, where he starred in football, basketball and track and field. He won the 1940 NCAA championship in the long jump at 24 ft. 10 1/4 in. At that time, in college, baseball was his "worst sport."

At age twenty-eight Jackie broke the color barrier in major league baseball in 1947, and won the Baseball Rookie of the Year award. Two years later he was the National League batting champion and Most Valuable Player. As a Brooklyn Dodger he was on three World Series teams playing several positions: first, second and third base and outfield, at all of which he had superb fielding percentages. His career offensive statistics are: batting average, .311; home runs, 137; RBI, 734; stolen bases, 197. Significantly, he was a fierce and fair competitor; perhaps the fiercest of all. But his spectacular athleticism merely added luster to his monumental humanism.

RENATA TEBALDI
b. February 1, 1922, Pesaro, Italy; d. 2004, San Marino, Italy

Renata Tebaldi, much beloved lyric-spinto soprano, possessed one of the most beautiful voices in opera and was said by Arturo Toscanini to have the voice of an angel. Though a dedicated artist, Tebaldi avoided singing French or German, preferring the beauty of her native Italian. She made her debut in Parma in *La Boheme* in 1944, in Trieste as Desdemona in 1946, and in the same year at La Scala in a concert conducted by Toscanini. She made her American debut in San Francisco in 1950 as Aida, and at the Metropolitan Opera in 1955 as Desdemona opposite Mario Del Monaco's Otello.

Tebaldi never married nor had children and devoted herself wholly to her singing, which can be appreciated on some of her best recordings, including: *Cavaleria rusticana* with Jussi Bjorling (London Records); *Andrea Chenier*, with Del Monaco and Fiorenza Cossotto (Decca); *Madama Butterfly*, with Carlo Bergonzi (Decca); *Tosca,* with Giuseppi di Stefano and *Tito Gobbi* (live from La Scala, Opera d'Oro); *Turandot*, with Birgit Nilsson and Bjorling (RCA); *Aida*, with Bergonzi and Giulietta Simionato (Decca Legends); and *Otello* with Del Monaco and Protti (Decca Legends).

FIDEL CASTRO

b. August 13, Birán Oriente, 1926 Cuba; d. 2016, Havana, Cuba

As a twenty-seven-yr-old lawyer, in 1953, Castro led a group of rebels against the dictatorship of Fulgencio Batista in an unsuccessful attack on the army's Moncada Barracks. Many of the rebels were killed or tortured. Castro and twenty-five comrades were imprisoned. At trial Castro defended himself in a speech, later published, called "History Will Absolve Me." After a year in prison Castro and others were released under a general amnesty. The great Uruguayan journalist, Eduardo Galeano, appraised the young defendant: "Castro has the look of a man who gives all of himself without asking anything in return...His words are not for the ones kissed by the gods; he speaks for the ones pissed on by the devils...Fidel claims the ancient right of rebellion against despotism."

In November, 1956, Fidel, his brother Raul and Che Guevara organized an expedition of eighty-one armed revolutionaries to attack Batista's government from Mexico. Over the next two and a half years the Castro brothers, Guevara and Camilo Cienfuegos led a guerrilla army from the Sierra Maestra of Oriente Province to Havana to overthrow the dictator. Castro was hailed internationally as a great revolutionary liberator and in Latin America as a warrior against North American imperialism.

Castro traveled to the U.S. to speak at the United Nations General Assembly and was greeted warmly by the general public that gathered in the area near his hotel in Manhattan, to which he was confined. But President Eisenhower, who in his administration had ordered the assassination of Jacobo Arbenz, Patrice Lumumba and Mohammad Mossadegh, declined to meet with the young liberator of Cuba. He also cancelled Cuba's sugar quota in 1960, setting in motion the first of many economic sanctions or "embargoes" designed to damage Cuba.

President Kennedy went further than Eisenhower, ordering on several separate occasions the assassination of Castro. Then, on April 16, 1961, the U.S. launched an invasion against Cuba at the Bay of Pigs, which was quickly defeated with Castro on the scene directing the defense. In October 1961, the USSR began shipping missiles bound for Cuba and the U.S. responded with a naval quarantine. The crisis passed when the USSR agreed to recover the missiles and the U.S. agreed not to invade Cuba. For the next fifty years Castro remained in power, out-living and out-smarting all his Cold War-imbued presidential adversaries. While the U.S. initiated wars against Vietnam, Cambodia, Grenada, Nicaragua and Iraq, and used its military might against other countries, Castro improved health care, education, and literacy in his own country.

RUTH BADER GINSBURG
b. March 15,1933, Brooklyn, New York City, NY

Ruth Bader Ginsburg, born to Russian-Jewish immigrants, became the second female justice confirmed to the U.S. Supreme Court when she was appointed by President Bill Clinton in 1993. Ginsburg attended Cornell University, then Harvard Law and Columbia Law School, earning law review honors at both schools and graduating in 1959.

From 1960-1962 she clerked for U.S. District Court, Southern District of New York, Judge Edmund L. Palmieri. From 1963-1972 she was a law professor at Rutgers School of Law. In 1970 she co-founded the Women's Rights Project at ACLU devoted exclusively to women's rights. In l972 she co-founded the Women's Rights Project at ACLU and in 1973 became ACLU's general counsel, a position in which she successfully argued a series of landmark cases before the U.S. Supreme Court extending equal rights for women. Her colleague, Justice Antonin Scalia, praised the work of Justice Ginsburg, saying, "she became the leading (and very successful) litigator on behalf of women's rights - the Thurgood Marshall of that cause, so to speak."

In 1980 President Jimmy Carter appointed Ginsburg to the U.S. Court of Appeals for the D.C. Circuit, and in 1983 she was elevated to the U.S. Supreme Court. Since then she has distinguished herself as the strongest dissenting voice on a court dominated by conservative, activist justices.

MUHAMMAD ALI
b. January 17, 1942, Louisville, KY; d. 2016, Scottsdale, AZ

Cassius Clay, better known as Muhammad Ali, a name he adopted after converting to Islam in 1964, is widely considered to be the greatest boxer of all time. At a height of 6'4", he danced around the ring with grace and speed, was quick, powerful and durable, and could out-talk opponents and journalists alike. He summed up his own style, saying he "floated like a butterfly and stung like a bee." He boasted that he was "The Greatest" and many boxing fans and sports fans with no special interest in boxing in countries around the world agreed.

Cassius Clay won the light heavyweight gold medal at the Olympic Games in Rome in 1960 when he was eighteen years old. Four years later, as a seemingly hopeless underdog, he defeated Sonny Liston to become the world heavyweight champion. Shortly thereafter, he converted to Islam, changed his name and refused to be inducted into the U.S. military. In one of the most cogent arguments against the draft and U.S. imperialism, Ali proclaimed he had no fight with the Viet Cong. He was convicted of avoiding the draft without cause and sentenced to five years in prison and banned from fighting for three years. Though he served none of the prison sentence, he lost almost four years of his prime fighting years. The U.S. Supreme Court ultimately reversed the appellate court decision against him in the case of *Clay vs. United States*. He reclaimed the heavyweight championship twice, in 1974 against Joe Frazier and in 1975 against George Foreman.

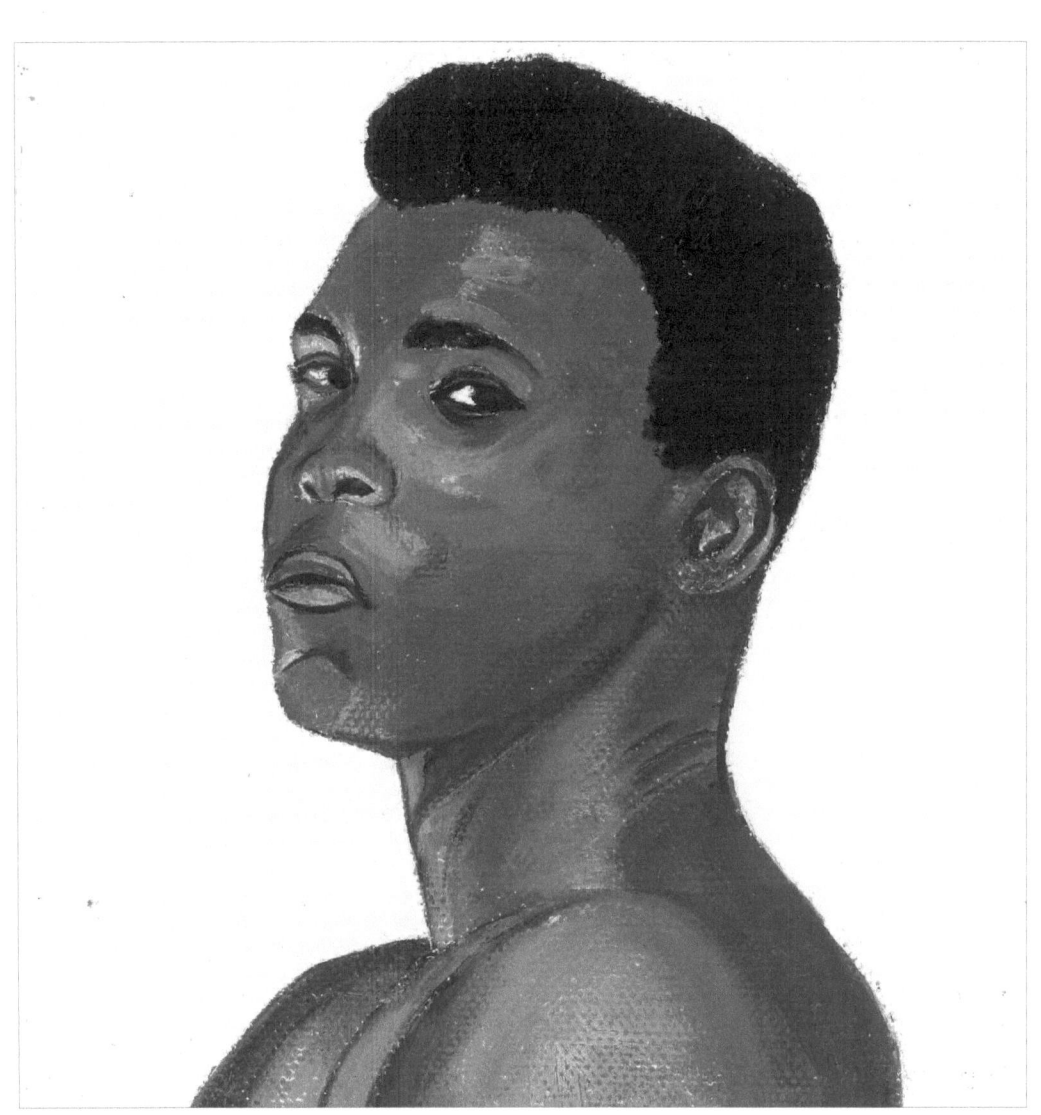

MARTIN LUTHER KING, JR.
b. January 15, 1929, Atlanta, GA; d. April 4, 1968, Memphis, TN

Martin Luther King Jr., a Baptist minister educated at Morehouse College, Crozer Theological Seminary and Boston University, was the most important civil rights activist of the 20th century. He led the social struggle to advance civil rights through tactics of nonviolence and civil disobedience. He was planning a national occupation of Washington, D.C. called the Poor People's Campaign when he was assassinated at age thirty-nine in Memphis.

King led the Montgomery bus boycott in 1955 and two years later became the first president of the Southern Christian Leadership Conference. In 1962 he led an unsuccessful campaign against segregation in Albany, Georgia. Then, in 1963 he helped Bayard Ruskin, Roy Wilkins, A. Philip Randolph, Whitney Young, John Lewis and James L. Farmer, Jr. organize the March on Washington, where he delivered his famous "I Have a Dream" speech. Shortly thereafter, with significant help from King, President Lyndon Johnson signed into law the Civil Rights Act of 1964. In 1965 he helped organize the Selma to Montgomery, Alabama marches.

He gradually turned his attention to the U.S. involvement in Southeast Asia. On April 4, 1967, at Riverside Church in New York City, he delivered what was probably the strongest speech by "anyone" against the war in Vietnam, in which he called the U.S. government "the greatest purveyor of violence in the world today."

ROGER FEDERER
b. August 8,1981, Basel, Switzerland

It is easy to think of Roger Federer as the perfect tennis player. Former tennis greats and tennis fans commonly opine that Federer is the best player ever. He stands 6 ft. 1 in., plays right handed, uses a one-hand backhand, serves with power and precision, speeds fluidly around the court, never seeming to tire or perspire and at age thirty-six continues to win Grand Slam events. He has won Wimbledon eight times, the French Open once, the U.S. Open five times, and the Australian Open six times.

He followed his idol, Pete Sampras, the top player of the 1990s, as the dominant player of the next decade, before sharing his dominance with younger rivals Rafael Nadal, Novak Djokovic and Andy Murray. He continued to play at or near the top for several years with the same grace, good sportsmanship and determination.

David Foster Wallace, brilliant writer and former top-notch junior tennis player, paid tribute to the man he considered to be the best tennis player by describing what he called a Federer Moment: "There are times, watching the young Swiss at play, when the jaw drops and eyes protrude and sounds are made that bring spouses in from other rooms to see if you're OK. The Moments are more intense if you've played enough tennis to understand the impossibility of what you have just seen him do."